Completing the Service

*Are You Ready and Willing to Earn
the Money You Deserve?*

Sheila J. Cline-Bass

iUniverse, Inc.
Bloomington

Completing the Service

iUniverse books may be ordered through booksellers or by contacting:

iUniverse
1663 Liberty Drive
Bloomington, IN 47403
www.iuniverse.com
1-800-Authors (1-800-288-4677)

Because of the dynamic nature of the Internet, any web addresses or links contained in this book may have changed since publication and may no longer be valid. The views expressed in this work are solely those of the author and do not necessarily reflect the views of the publisher, and the publisher hereby disclaims any responsibility for them.

Any people depicted in stock imagery provided by Thinkstock are models, and such images are being used for illustrative purposes only.

Certain stock imagery © Thinkstock.

ISBN: 978-1-4620-6642-1 (sc)
ISBN: 978-1-4620-6643-8 (e)

Printed in the United States of America

iUniverse rev. date: 12/14/2011

This book is dedicated to many people:

First and foremost I thank God for the life He has blessed me with and the gifts He has seen fit to grant me. Everything I do will forever be for His glory.

To my husband, Ted Bass, and our son, Logan, for all of your support and encouragement. The love, laughter, and life we share will be forever blessed.

To my parents, Bill and Peggy Cline, for the love, support, and drive you have given me. You have taught me well that, in whatever I do, I should strive to be the best at it that I can be. You have both inspired my life and instilled the best values. You are the best parents anyone could possibly hope for.

To the rest of my family—in-laws, blood relations, and extended members—and my many wonderful friends. My life would not be complete without you all. (Or should I say "all y'all"?)

To Pam Rohner Swart and Connie Swenson, my COS school friends and sisters, who have been such sources of inspiration to me and the best of friends.

To Angie and Jeremy Scheff, my partners and friends. You are constant sources of joy, and you never fail to back me up on anything. Your unwavering support and your willingness to assist me in "testing" my theories are the things I depend on every day.

To Julie Molacek, Chris Rieckman, Debi Decker, and Patty Kopp for your support, insight, and advice. I will be forever grateful to have you in my life.

To Darla Quimby for always making me look great!

To Dave King and Shelly Sowada for always knowing there was something more for me and never failing to remind me of that.

To the memories of Linda Traulich and Jan Holien. Linda, you were one of the most encouraging people I have ever had the pleasure of knowing. Jan, to me, you were the best color instructor in the world. You ladies are truly missed.

And last, but most certainly not least, this book is dedicated to the memory of my daughter, Morgan Leigh Cline, who on November 12, 2008, at the age of seventeen, was hit by a drunk driver and went home to be with our Lord and Savior. Morgan, you will forever be in my heart. You were constantly pushing for me to write this book and build the Transformations Salon Consulting website. I only regret that I was never able to tell you in person how much you inspired me. I will always love you and will see you again when I get home to Heaven. Mommy loves you!

Contents

Chapter One

Welcome to My World

Hello and welcome to my world. My name is Sheila J. Cline-Bass, and I am the owner of Transformations Salon Consulting. Let me get right to the point: this book was written just for you, the salon professional. It is my sincere hope that this book will assist you in taking your business to the next level—through retailing.

As a licensed cosmetologist and former distributor sales consultant (also known as an account executive or sales rep), I have had the privilege of working with many wonderful people in the beauty industry. From these people I learned many valuable lessons regarding retail sales in the salon. With those lessons I was able to achieve top retail sales in my salon, and I later developed the retail sales program that I lay out in this book. This in turn afforded me the opportunity to assist many other salons in achieving their goals in retail sales.

While this does not make me an expert by any means, my experience did show me that—even with so many sales programs available—people were still not getting it. It seemed that every program out there was too product specific, too extensive, or too expensive. I can't tell you how many stylists and salon owners told me that after purchasing a retail sales "program" that cost anywhere from $300 to $600, they did not have the time to get all the way through the four to six CDs or DVDs and workbooks. In essence, they did not have the time or money to invest in using a program they did not have the time or money for. Make sense?

So, I decided to use the information I gathered and a method I'm sure you have all heard of: the KISS method. Yes, the "keep it simple s_____" (sweetheart, stupid . . . insert your own *S* word here) method to assist you in learning the power, procedure, and profit potential of retail sales.

I must take the time to explain that this is something I am very passionate about. The reason is that I have seen firsthand the difference it can make in the attitudes and success of many salon owners and stylists. My method is an easy and powerful way to enhance your business. If you are reading this, it must be because you have a desire to learn as well.

Personally, when I was in the salon in 2001, there was a particular product line that I *loved*! Seeing how passionate I was about it, my then boss, Chris Rieckman, told me that I should think about working with the distribution company. That way I could get the product line into every salon and, by doing so, get it into the hands of many more clients. Two weeks later we heard that our rep for that company was quitting. The rest is history.

Again, it is my sincere hope that you will find this book insightful, educational, and maybe a little entertaining. This book should take less than two hours to read. So, grab a cup of coffee (or a latté, hot chocolate, chai, cucumber water, or whatever you serve in your salon!), put up your feet, and let's learn some stuff and enjoy doing it.

Oh, I almost forgot! The most important thing: this is your book! You will be asked to write in it. Grab a pen and a highlighter, and let's get to it!

Chapter Two

The Stinking Thinking of Salon Retail Sales

Every time I'm working with a salon and ask the employees how well they do with retail sales, it seems to open up a litany of excuses. Some of my favorites are:

- I'm not *trained* to sell.
- I'm not sure which *products* to offer.
- Selling retail *does not* help my business.
- Selling retail only helps the *salon owner.*
- I don't have *time* to sell.

So, first things first: take a couple of minutes and rate yourself (I told you to grab a pen!). Be honest. How well do you think you do selling retail in the salon? Rate yourself on a scale of one to ten. Are you a one (never sold anything)? Are you a five (only when I think about it)? Or are you a ten (you should be selling ice cubes in Antarctica)? Write that number below.

I am a _____ at selling retail.

If you rated yourself between one and seven, you are in the right place! If you rated yourself between eight and ten, you are also in the right place. Why? Because we never stop learning, that's why. Even if you are great at salon retail sales, you will be able to improve your techniques and thereby increase your retail-to-service ratio by an additional 10 percent or more.

There is a huge misconception regarding retail sales in the salon industry today. Many people think that selling retail is an option. Well, guess what? It's not! Selling retail is a vital part of salon service.

However, the average stylist is not trained in retail. So the excuse becomes "I don't know how to sell!" So, so, so true! I remember cosmetology school. Not one day did we spend *learning* how to sell. So, here is what you do: *stop* trying to sell! Instead, you need to be:

COMPLETING THE SERVICE!

You do realize that is the title of this book. Well, that addresses not being trained to sell, but I'm sure you're asking, "What about the other excuses?" Yes, yes, I know. Let's break those down.

"I'm not sure which products to offer."

Let me give you a few quick tips on this one. When working in salons, most stylists fall head over heels in love with a few products. These products usually end up being the stylist's best sellers, with good reason. If you love something, your love or passion for it comes through in the way you present it. Let me give you an example:

> *There is a story of a man who loved diamonds. He searched the world over for the most beautiful he could find. One day, he met a diamond merchant who eventually became his best source for his beloved gems. This man was extremely diligent in locating the best for his clients.*

> *One day, the merchant contacted his new best client and informed him that he located a diamond that would rival anything else this man had in his collection. "Would you like to see it?" he asked his client. "But, of course I would!" the gentleman responded, "I'll be in later today!"*

> *Later that day the gentleman eagerly went into the diamond shop, only to find the diamond merchant preoccupied with another client. However, the sales manager was available and would be happy to show the man the diamond. The sales manager then began to describe every technical detail of the diamond. When he was done with his description, the gentleman politely thanked him and started to leave.*

Having witnessed the gentleman beginning to leave the diamond merchant excused himself from his other client and went to the gentleman and asked why he was leaving. "Well, I'm not particularly interested in that diamond." the gentleman replied. "Would you allow me to show you the diamond again?" asked the diamond merchant. "I'm not sure what good that would do, but if you must." replied the gentleman.

The diamond merchant didn't repeat one thing the sales manager had said. He simply cupped the diamond in his hands, stared at it, and began to describe the beauty of the stone in a way that revealed why this stone stood out from all the others he had seen in his life. When he was finished, he placed the diamond lovingly on the black velvet pallet and turned to the gentleman. "I'll take it!" the gentleman said.

Then tucking his new purchase into his breast pocket, he commented to the merchant, "Sir, I wonder why you were able to sell me the diamond when your salesman could not?"

The merchant replied, "That sales manager is the best in the business. He knows more about diamonds than anyone, including myself and I pay him a large salary for his knowledge and expertise. But I would gladly pay him twice as much if I could put into him something I have which he lacks. You see, he knows diamonds, but I love them."

(Story Adapted from Hot Illustrations for Youth Talks by Wayne Rice, Copyright © 1993 Youth Specialties, Zondervan Publishing House.)

So, start with the products you love and learn how those products affect different hair types. The secret to product knowledge is this: learn one product line very well, and everything else will fall into place. Why? Well, all product lines are similar in their offerings (they strengthen, straighten, moisturize, add volume, color protect, etc.). In skin care there are products for dry, oily, and combination skin as well as products with anti-aging properties. In nail products, there are items for dry/brittle, oily, and normal nails. See a pattern here? You must take the time to *learn* about the products that are being offered.

"Selling retail does not help my business."

In chapters 3 and 7 we will discuss the financial impact that selling retail has on your business, as an individual stylist and as a salon owner. Needless to say, selling retail equals more money and better client retention—ergo, more money for you, the individual.

"Selling retail only helps the salon owner."

Again, in chapters 3 and 7 we will address this further. However, if you are in a salon that does not offer commissions based on retail sales, talk to the salon owner about offering an incentive for you to sell retail. If they won't, your best bet is to *find another salon*! There are plenty of wonderful salons out there that offer great commissions on services and retail.

"I don't have time to sell."

This is probably the number one excuse I hear from stylists about why they don't sell retail in the salon. Well, here is my complete unbiased opinion on that one: if you can do a haircut and style in thirty minutes, then you have thirty minutes to sell retail. Keep control of the situation and the conversation and be professional.

Chapter Three

Why Sell Retail?

Before I explain why you should sell retail, I'll give you the top four reasons people don't sell retail. Just to clarify, these statistics are based on national sales statistics. In other words, these numbers come from every given sales situation. Basically these numbers cover everything that could possibly be sold, from aardvarks to zucchini.

National statistics have revealed the following reasons why salespeople fail:

1. <u>Fifteen percent</u> fail because of improper training in product and sales skills.
2. <u>Twenty percent</u> fail because of poor verbal and written communication skills.
3. <u>Fifteen percent</u> fail because of poor/problematic bosses or management.
4. <u>Fifty percent</u> fail because of poor *attitude*.

Ask yourself, "Which category am I in?"

Write your answer here: _____

If you are in the improper-training category, you're in luck—you have this book. This book will assist you in learning how to properly present products to your clients so that they *will* purchase. If you are lacking in product knowledge, understand this: the only thing stopping you from learning about the products is you. Product knowledge can be obtained very easily. Practically every product line manufacturer has a website that is full of information on each product. Most distributors have sales sheets on their product offering, and many run classes on them as well. Your

DSC (distributor sales consultant) or the salespeople at your distributor store (wherever you purchase your product) are trained in each and every product line they carry. They should be more than helpful at demonstrating how to present the products. And last but not least, every single product has a description on the back of the bottle. *Read it!*

If you are in the poor verbal and written communication skills category, again, you're in luck. Later in this book I will give you some great key questions to ask your clients and some wonderful ways to combat objections that your clients may have. The secret to learning how to communicate with other people properly is to find someone who communicates well and ask for their advice.

If you are in the poor/problematic bosses or management category—say it with me—you're in luck! Yes, sad but true, there are some bosses out there who should never have become bosses. They are irritable, snotty, and just plain unhappy. The best thing you can do is shine. Be a model employee. If you ever hope to have your own salon one day, this will teach you how *not* to treat people. If you want the best employees, don't repeat the actions of a poor boss.

Sidebar here: Being a great boss does not mean you need to be everyone's friend. You are there to guide the employees to ensure the success of the business. Sometimes that means making tough decisions that ultimately make someone mad. It brings to mind something that I heard the great comedian Robin Williams say: "You can only please some of the people some of the time and just piss the rest off!"

Secondary sidebar: If you are self-employed and this is your problem … Well, you may want to have a conversation with yourself about the issues. Keep in mind that if you talk to yourself, you are not crazy. If you talk to yourself and ask yourself questions, you are not crazy. If you talk to yourself, ask questions, and then answer them, you are still *not* crazy. However, if you talk to yourself, ask yourself questions, and then respond, "Huh?" You may want to seek professional help.

Lastly, if you are in the poor attitude category … Well, you're probably not reading this book. These people are not your typical career people. They show up late, leave early, actually take a lunch break, and constantly watch the clock. They couldn't care less about the business and just want a paycheck. I honestly believe half of the people that rated in the poor/problematic bosses category should have been placed in this one. I have met many stylists who blame their own bad attitudes on their bosses. "She doesn't understand me!" "She doesn't like me!" These are the people you always want to ask, "Would you like a little cheese with that whine?" They don't do anything to assist the salon owner or manager. They talk about themselves to their clients constantly, never pre-book, and never, ever sell retail. They follow the misconceptions that selling retail is an option and that it only helps the salon owner and not them. They won't take the time to further their education. They consider a hair show a vacation; they party the whole time and never attend classes.

My advice to any salon owner or manager who has this person on staff is *get rid of them*! You know the old saying, "One bad apple can spoil the whole barrel." I have personally witnessed one stylist almost completely destroy three different salons. Trust me—there are dedicated people out there.

While I was in cosmetology school, my friends Pam and Connie and I were all considered nontraditional students. I'm assuming that meant we'd had lives prior to attending the school. I don't like to think it meant we were *older*! Anyway, our class had thirty-two students registered at the start of the spring semester. After two weeks, we were down to twenty-five. After the second semester we were down to eighteen, and by the time we graduated, we had five. All of the instructors asked me if I thought our class had dropped off by so many because of them. I had to reply, *"Absolutely not!"*

We were truly blessed with some of the best instructors in the world (at least that was our opinion). Connie, Pam, and I then had to explain to our instructors that the reason was actually us mothering the rest of the class. We could tell many of the girls were not serious about cosmetology. They considered it an "out" career. Their attitude was "I'm going to school for something so that my parents will shut up." The problem was that my friends and I were extremely passionate about cosmetology and wanted to learn without interruptions. Plus, as mothers, we were sick and tired of watching these people waste their parents' money. We successfully placed five students in accounting, seven in photography, and two in criminal justice, and sent one on a backpacking trip through Europe. The rest we just sent home to their moms.

Now that that's out of the way, let's discuss the top five reasons why we *should* sell retail.

5. You are a professional.
4. Customers need and use product.
3. Selling retail supports the industry.
2. Selling retail increases salon profits.
1. **Selling retail increases client retention!**

So again, let's break each one of these points down:

You are a professional.

We will cover this particular point in depth in the next chapter. For the time being, please understand that *you are a professional.* A professional makes sure every *i* is dotted and every *t* is crossed. If a client comes to your salon for a service and they are willing to pay their hard-earned money for that service, they should also be willing to *pay for the insurance to guarantee that service.* And, you need to explain that to them.

If you have ever purchased a new car, you know they will tell you what type of oil to use for that make and model. So, would you go out and buy cooking oil instead? Of course not!

Customers need and use product.

People use shampoo—and at least two-thirds of those people use conditioner also. Additionally, at least two-thirds use at least one styling product.

Selling retail supports the industry.

Clients need to buy these products. Nothing is free, and most people do not make their own product. So, where are they going to get it? Some will buy product in a professional salon; others will go to a grocery store, department store, or drug store.

Offering these products in salons cuts down on diversion. Yes, I said it! The big *D* word. I know, I know — touchy subject. However, what you need to understand is why products are diverted: there is a market for it. If you are not prescribing and offering professional retail products in your salon, you are driving those sales to the diverted product stores and the over-the-counter market because your clients want and need them.

Selling retail increases salon profits.

Selling retail increases salon profits. Yes, indeed it does. If you are not sure just how, let me take you through an example:

- The national average profit on salon services is between 5 and 7 percent.
  $25.00 haircut @ 7 percent profit margin = $1.75 profit.
- The national average profit on a retail sale is 23 percent.
  $25.00 retail sale @ 23 percent profit margin = $5.75 profit.
- **$8.00 retail sale @ 23 percent profit margin = $1.92
  (This is greater than the profit on a $25.00 haircut.)**

In summary—highlight, underline, and circle this:

Every lost retail dollar should be compared to a lost service client!

Let's take a quick look at what the value of an average cut/color client is:

- Haircut and Style @ $25 × 8 visits per year = $200 in revenue
- Highlight or Color @ $55 × 8 visits per year = $440 in revenue
- Wax (brow and lip) @ $16 × 8 visits per year = $128 in revenue
- Retail (average *) @ $50 × 8 visits per year = $400 in revenue
  (*for shampoo, conditioner, styling product, and hairspray)

Total average value of a client for one year = $1,168

But remember: one client will usually refer at least two friends.
3 Clients × $1,168 = $3,504

And each client will usually stay with a stylist for an average of three to five years.
$3,504 (value of three clients) × 5 years = $17,520.00

Remember these figures each time a client walks in your door!

Selling retail increases client retention.

Now that you understand what your clients are worth, don't you want to keep them? Absolutely! So, yes, retaining your clients is the number one reason you should sell retail. But seriously, don't just take my word for it. In every single beauty-industry-related retail class I have been in, these statistics have been explained. Why? Because industry studies have shown that people are loyal to those whom they deem to be experts.

- Sell a client one product, and they are 30 percent more likely to remain loyal.
- Sell a client two products, and they are 50 percent more likely to remain loyal.
- Sell a client three products, and they are 95 percent more likely to remain loyal.

Clients are more likely to purchase products in salons rather than the general market if they feel their stylists have their best interests in mind when recommending products.

So, ask yourself, "Why would a client leave my salon?" If you don't know the answer to that, here are some statistics that answer that very question. These statistics come from a survey conducted by the Matrix® Corporation in 2007 but still hold true today.

Why do clients leave?
- One percent pass away.
- Three percent move away.

- Five percent know someone else in the industry.
- Nine percent are lost to competitors (coupons, flyers, support at schools, etc.).
- Fourteen percent are not satisfied. (Note: I truly believe this category should be split into two parts. Seven percent are not satisfied with you, the salon, etc. The other 7 percent are not satisfied with anything! They are just completely negative people, and no one can satisfy them. These are people you *do not* want as clients!)
- Sixty-eight percent *feel* that you no longer care about them!

Why do the clients in this last group feel this way? Because *you*:
- don't make them *feel* special when you greet them;
- don't *suggest* new styles;
- don't *show* them how to style their hair;
- already have their *color* mixed up before they walk in the door (my biggest pet peeve);
- *disappear* while they are processing;
- don't *recommend* hair care products; or
- don't *show* them how to use the products that you are recommending.

You can ensure that they never feel that way, if you take the time to:
- *call* them three to five days after the service to find out how they like it;
- send a *thank you* card after service;
- send birthday cards with "Birthday Wishes" *coupons*;
- *reward* referrals (give clients a reason to send their friends to you!);
- call clients that you have not seen in *four* months;
- *attend* classes/shows (bring back the *excitement* and ideas!); and
- offer proper *maintenance* products for home use and *show* them how to use them.

Here is another question: Should you guarantee a service if the client does not purchase the prescribed support products from you? Absolutely not! You do not know what products they are using at home, so how can you guarantee the service? If a client is using a product at home that has the pH of floor cleaner, will it hold her hair color? *No!* If you give a client a great cut and style and she is using incorrect product, incorrectly, will she be happy? *No!* The thing to remember here is that, if this happens, the client is going to blame you! When I've interviewed salon clients and asked if they use salon products, many of them tell me no, because their stylist either a) did not recommend product, or b) recommended product but did not show the client how to use it.

My advice is to post a policy stating your guarantee. If you're not sure how to go about it, use this:

SALON POLICY
It is the policy of this salon not to guarantee <u>any</u> salon service unless the proper maintenance products and equipment, <u>sold by this salon</u>, are being used by the client to maintain the services provided.

That one paragraph covers all your bases: retail products, treatments, and tools. So, if you are not carrying a line of professional tools … get one!

Chapter Four

Who's a Professional?

As many of you know, this industry has run the gamut in terms of how it is viewed by the general public. Not so many years ago, professionals in the industry were viewed as being in a "servant" position. Hairstylists were treated as second-class citizens. They were told what to do by their clients and wouldn't even think about striking up a personal conversation.

Then, in the late sixties and early seventies, things began to change. With the introduction of "wash and wear" hairstyles came a paradigm shift in that prior perception. Beauty professionals began recommending styles and products, and the industry took on a more professional image.

This brought on an onslaught of product manufacturers and new styling techniques, all of which has brought us to where we are today: a multibillion-dollar industry with constantly changing technology in chemical processes, tools, techniques, and products.

The question to ask yourself is this: Is this a professional industry?

If you are unsure about how to the answer to that question, try answering these questions first:

1. Did you go to *school* to learn the trade?
2. Did you *graduate*?
3. Did you take a test to get a *license*?
4. Did you *pass*?
5. Do you now *provide services* to clients in a salon that also has a *license*?
6. Does the state in which you provide these services also *regulate* the industry?

If you answered yes to those questions, then, guess what? You are a professional in a professional industry! The three major components that make up a professional industry are (highlight these!):

1. Education
2. Licensing
3. Regulation

Now ask yourself this: Why do my clients come to me? Really put some thought into this one. Do they come to you because they are family or friends and feel obligated? Do they come because you know all the latest gossip in town? Do they come because they know you are well educated and will listen to their needs and perform a great service? (Write your answer below.)

Why do my clients come to me?

_____

_____

_____

Now, let's think about the impact we make as professionals in this industry by comparing what we do to another professional, multibillion-dollar industry: the medical field. I know some of you are thinking that this is a bit of a stretch, but let me take you through the similarities through the eyes of a four-year-old.

I had this adorable little girl come into the salon for a haircut. She was about four years old and just the cutest little thing you will ever see. But, she was very small for her age. This child had had the most unimaginable first four years of life. First, she was born very premature and then, when she was two years old, was involved in an accident in which the car she was riding in was hit by a train.

In her life to that point she had been in and out of hospitals since the day she was born. So, when I say she was small, I mean tiny for a four-year-old. The only way we could get her into the shampoo bowl was to roll the nail table over, lay her on it, and have her mother help hold her head.

When we got done shampooing and I took her to my station, I had a conversation with her regarding what she wanted done with her hair (confirming with her mother over her head).

As I began cutting her hair, she informed me that she had just gotten a new puppy (named Puppy), had a cat (named Kitty), and hated trains (understandably). When I finished the cut, I sprayed a little glitter in her hair, put a pretty little bow in, and—I kid you not—she looked like an angel. I gave her a piece of candy, booked her next appointment, and told her that I had enjoyed meeting her. At that point, she smiled at me and said "Thank you, doctor!" (Awwww ... how sweet!)

I told her that I wasn't a doctor, to which she replied, "Yes, you are." I was taken aback by this but didn't say any more.

On her next visit she walked in the door with a huge grin on her cherub face, walked right up, grabbed my leg, and said "Hello, doctor!" (Again, awwwww!)

I asked her mother why she thought I was a doctor. Her mother answered, "Think about it from her perspective: She has seen a lot of doctors in her life. She comes to see you because she has a problem with her hair. You talk to her about it, confirm it with me, fix the problem, give her candy, and always tell her it was nice to see her. Plus, you wear a "lab coat" and have shiny tools. To her, you do the same thing her regular doctor does." Wow!

That encounter totally changed the way I view this industry. So, are we "hair doctors"? Absolutely!

When you go to the doctor, you go for one of two reasons: either there is something wrong, or you need a checkup. People go to the cosmetologist for of one of two reasons: either there is something wrong (maybe they tried to do it themselves, or a friend did it for them), or they need maintenance (cut, color or perm, facial, nails, and so on).

Once a doctor goes through the checkup process, explains what is wrong, and makes recommendations for treatment, he or she whips out a little pad and writes down the information needed to cure said problem.

Once a cosmetologist goes through the process, explains what is wrong, and makes recommendations for treatment (cut, color or perm, facial, or nail care), he or she then—*Stop!*

At the doctor's office, we take that little piece of paper to the pharmacy and give it to someone who can actually read it (one of life's great mysteries). They then take it to the back of the room and come out a few minutes later with a little bag, hand it to us, and *we pay for it*! We then take our little bag home, open it, pull the little bottle out, and read the label. What does it say? Use as directed! Duh!

In the salon, we completely lose it at this point and say something like, "Do you need anything today?" The answer we usually get is a no. Come on! That's like asking someone, "Do you want fries with that?" when they didn't order any.

Another great mystery of life is why we do that. One of the main reasons is that, as we have discussed earlier, we are not taught how to prescribe products to our customers. Nor do we (truly) understand why we should. And often—and this just floors me—we are *afraid* to do it or don't think we have the *right* to do it.

Since we have established the fact that we are professionals in a professional industry, should we not also agree that our responsibility to our clients is to indeed complete the service?

Again, think of your doctor. Imagine you had a problem that he discovered but was afraid to tell you about. What do you think your reaction would be when you eventually found out? Can you say "malpractice"?

You must be willing to constantly view yourself as a professional. And, yes, you can be a professional and still have a lot of fun.

The easiest way to be successful in business and in life is to set goals for what you want.

Chapter Five

So ... What Is a Goal?

(And Why Do I Want One?)

Many people have told me they don't set goals because they never reach them. Okay, this tells me one of two things is happening: either they are setting their goals too high or they do nothing to try to reach those goals.

You have to understand that setting goals is a road map to success: a mini business plan, if you will. They are imperative if you truly want to succeed. Goal setting and achievement are self-disciplines that have to be practiced every single day. Would you drive cross-country without gas money, insurance information, clothes, and some idea of how to get to your destination? Unless someone else is paying for it, doing the driving, and purchasing you a new outfit every time you stop, probably not.

National studies reveal that only 5 percent of salespeople set goals. This information is based on the sales industry as a whole. My guess would be that maybe only 1 percent of stylists actually set service and retail goals in the salon. Many people who do not set goals in their personal lives will still set goals in their business lives and have no problem following through.

One of my friends from cosmetology school, Pam, set a few goals for herself. She wanted to finish school, get her hours for her manager's license, get married, open her own salon, and have a baby—in that order! Did she achieve those goals? Absolutely! And yes, she achieved them in that order.

As a matter of fact, she graduated second in her class (after me). She then went to work in a very nice spa in the area. She met a wonderful man and married him after the appropriate year of dating and engagement. She was pregnant in less than a year after that, opened an extremely successful salon in her home, and then she gave birth to a beautiful little girl. Currently, she has one of the most successful salons in the area.

Now, I have another friend who only sees the end result of goals. In other words, she dreams really big—but has no follow-through. She set a goal to purchase a brand new car within a year. At that point she had a great job with a good income and she had some money set aside for a down payment. Great!

When the year mark rolled around, guess what? She got her new car—but she ended up paying *way* more that she had anticipated because she had not set a financial goal along with her personal goal. Instead she had left the money she had in savings (and we all know how much interest we earn there). She never put any more aside, even after receiving a substantial raise in income, nor did she shop around for the best deal.

The end result was that she paid more than she could afford and ended up selling the car the next year and buying a smaller more economical car.

Had she set her goals properly, she would have realized that she needed more money down to keep her payments lower. Actually, if she had put the money she had in her savings account into a twenty-four-month CD, set aside what she had planned for a payment for twenty-four months, and purchased the previous year's model from a different dealer, she would have been able to pay *cash* for the car and would have had no monthly payment at all!

Are you starting to see why you need to set goals? They can help you achieve anything. But remember, they are just goals. If you do not reach them, it's okay—adjust them! If you want to be a millionaire—and who doesn't?—it's not going to happen in a year. (Not unless you are a hard-core gambler with a lot of luck.)

Take baby steps. Set two or three small goals—for example purchasing a new outfit or taking a weekend getaway—and then plan out how to make them happen. Write out your steps and follow through. Do your due diligence. Check prices, availability, whether items are going on sale, and so on. Break down the cost of your purchase: "If I save twenty-five dollars per week for four weeks I can buy that new …" Do that for whatever it is that you want—sweater, purse, spa service, shoes (Shoes? Did someone say shoes?!).

If you blow it one week and don't put away your twenty-five dollars, is your goal shot? *Absolutely not!* Reset your goal to five weeks. To help you get started setting your goals, take some time to write out a few basic goals. In the final chapter of this book, "Tips and Snips," you will find actual steps to help you in writing a goal along with a goal-setting worksheet.

And remember this: *A goal without a plan is just a wish.*

What are your goals?

Personal: _____

_____

Professional: _____

_____

Financial: _____

_____

Spiritual/charitable: _____

_____

A note about the spiritual/charitable goals: Most people don't know it, but in the Bible we are commanded to give. We are also commanded to love one another, and to believe in the Lord Jesus Christ and to have faith (yes, in addition to the Ten Commandments, there are other commands). Just consider this as well, the word *believe* is mentioned in the Bible 272 times, *faith* is mentioned 375 times, and *love* is mentioned 714 times. However, the word *give* is mentioned 2,162 times. Which one do you think God wants to make sure we understand?

(Reference from Better Together – What on Earth are we here for? video series by Pastor Rick Warren, Copyright © 2004, PurposeDriven Publishing)

Once you have written out your goals, make three or four copies. Keep one with you at all times (maybe in your wallet, on a photo keychain, or in your address book). Put two where you will see them every day. I always recommend the bathroom mirror and the refrigerator door because these are two places we are always looking. Finally, give a copy to someone you trust (like your spouse, parent, pastor, teacher, boss, or best friend,). Heck, give one to all of them!

Taking the time to state your goals ensures your future success. A study of Harvard Law graduates conducted in 1962 showed that 33 percent of the students wrote down their goals. Twenty years later, out of that 33 percent, 100 percent of them had achieved their goals. In fact, 98 percent had exceeded their goals. (Unfortunately, the other two percent had passed away.)

Now let's look at how to set a goal for the amount of retail you want to sell. These numbers are *not* based on any average salon or stylist; however, the 25 percent retail-to-service ratio is the national average. So you *always* want to use it as your minimum! A blank copy of this formula is also located in the "Tips and Snips" chapter.

Average number of clients per week: 40
    (Include all clients)

Average service ticket: $30.00
    (Total receipts for services ÷ number of clients)

Average total weekly gross service sales: = $1200.00
    (40 clients x $30.00 per client)

Retail to service percentage target: 25 percent
    (Set this number to what you wish to achieve)

Dollar retail goal per week: = $300.00
    ($1200.00 x 25 percent)

Dollar retail goal per client: = $7.50
   ($300.00 ÷ 40 average clients per week)

So, your goal is to sell $7.50 worth of retail to *every* client.

People often ask me these questions:

Have you always met your goals?   No.

Have you readjusted them?   Yes.

Will you give up?   No.

Do you still write them down? More now than ever!

The need to achieve goals and the drive behind them takes *focus*. Focus creates intensity, desire, and commitment. Stay focused on the end result.

Now, let's take it one step further. At first glance the next page appears blank—but at the very top there is a quote. On this page I want you to write a brief story of where you will be in five to ten years. When you have finished this, tear it out and make copies, just as you did with your goals list. Let everyone you come across know where you want to be. Chances are someone who knows what your goals are will help you achieve them.

"My dream is the birthplace of my future!"

Most experts agree that the only way to achieve success is to focus on the end result. Establish your goal, determine a plan of action, and stick with it until your goal is reached.

How can you stay focused? There are seven principles to follow to ensure that focus:

1. **Stop blaming circumstances for *your* situation.**
   The economy is down." "The weather has been bad."
   Those things may be true, but you have a choice in everything you do. Choose a better way.

2. **Stop blaming other people for *your* situation.**
   "It's not my job—it's hers!" "She doesn't like me!"
   Take responsibility for yourself and your actions. It's called accountability.

3. **Get to know your customer or prospect better every day.**
   It is just as easy to prevent problems as to handle them. You are always looking for solutions for your clients' issues with their hair, skin, and nails, so get to know their lifestyles so that you can better predict what their upcoming issues will be.

4. **Persist until you gain the answer you want.**
   A prospect will respect a tenacious salesperson. Do whatever it takes to hang in there! There is a wonderful saying that goes like this: "People who say no don't know enough." This basically means that when your client says no, he really means, "Tell me more."

5. **Know where you are or where you should be.**
   Manage your time. Show up fifteen minutes early for work. Make sure all sanitation is taken care of before leaving. Keep perfect records. Write as much information as you can about each client's visit.

6. **Work on your skills every day.**
Tapes, books, seminars, and product-knowledge information are your friends. The more you know, the less fear you'll have. *Knowledge is power!*

7. **Become solution oriented.**
Instead of complaining about your problems, take the same amount of time to work on solutions!

Once you have developed the focus level you need to achieve your goals, you must also learn how to turn potential into profit. The easiest way to do that is to follow the next four steps outlined here. These steps are actually daily reminders of what your end result can be.

First, you must anticipate the future. No matter how successful we are, without updating our working habits, we get into a rut. How many stylists do you know whose entire client base looks the same? They all have the same cut, color, and style. I don't know about you, but that scares me. One of the reasons stylists get into that rut is that they don't know what's going on in the industry.

Second, work from your client's agenda. If I told you, "Buy my book because I need a vacation really badly," you would probably say "No!"—or "Okay … if you take me with you!" (Now, I'm not saying that I wouldn't love to take everyone with me, but I just can't afford to.) However, if I said to you, "By purchasing this book and following the plan, you can achieve *your* goal of going to the Bahamas," you would probably be more apt to purchase it. The reason is that the purchase would benefit *you*.

Third, determine a plan of action and commit to it. Develop that take-charge attitude that so many people tell me they wish they had. Learn to keep control of the conversation that is going on with your client.

Fourth, understand and know your client's needs and meet them. We asked ourselves earlier why our customers come to see us. If, in your case, it is truly because you are a professional and have had open communication with your clients, then you should know before their next visit exactly what they need. I will take you through this with a little more detail in chapter 8.

People who track sales statistics say that it's all a numbers game. Well, if that is true, then remember this:

$$SW^3$$

Which stands for:

Some will.
Some won't.
So what?
Next!

Don't dwell on the numbers.

Chapter Six

Why Do People Buy?

They say that in sales it takes seven no's to get one yes. So, are you going to get that from one client?

	YOU	CLIENT
1.	"Do you want it?"	"No."
2.	"Do you want it?"	"No."
3.	"Do you want it?"	"No."
4.	"Do you want it?"	"No."
5.	"Do you want it?"	"No."
6.	"Do you want it?"	"No."
7.	"Do you want it?"	"No."
8.	"Do you want it?"	"Yes!"

It's not gonna happen! That looks more like harassment.

However, if you continually recommend a particular style, service, or product specifically for a client, might they eventually purchase it? Absolutely! The reason is they will eventually understand that you truly care about them and their skin, hair, and nails. There is an old saying that goes, "People don't care how much you know until they know how much you care." I have never heard a truer statement. If you take the time to find out why people buy things, you'll find it is usually because someone took a genuine interest in them, their needs, their situation, and so on. Put yourself in your client's situation: Is there any reason why (if you were the client) you would buy something from you (the stylist) based on the way you work with your clients?

In all actuality, there are only two reasons why people buy something. They either need it or want it. However, there are seven principles behind why people decide to purchase the specific item they select. In other words, this is how people buy based on the want or need.

They purchase based on:

- **Product warranty:** Does the manufacturer back up the product?
- **Service:** Does the product do what it was intended to do?
- **Convenience:** Is it right there when I want or need it? (I don't want to shop around.)
- **Price:** Is it affordable?
- **Selection:** Is there more than one brand to choose from?
- **Satisfaction guarantee:** Does the store back up the product?
- **Quality:** Is it good for the price?

Take a couple of minutes now and rank these in order of importance. Starting with what you think would be the least important. Think about the way you purchase things. Especially the way you would purchase items for yourself.

List them here:

7. _____
6. _____
5. _____
4. _____
3. _____
2. _____
1. _____

Want to see how you did? In chapter 10, "Tips and Snips," you will find the answer key. Don't cheat and look there before completing this exercise! It's important for you to learn this information so that you better understand the purchasing habits of your clients.

Rewrite the corrected list here:

7. _____

6. _____

5. _____

4. _____

3. _____

2. _____

1. _____

Now let's add one more thing to that mix: a recommendation. Think again about how you purchase. Would you even apply these seven principles if the product were recommended? Usually, it becomes more of a clarifier. In essence, it adds urgency to a need. "I need it" becomes "I need it *now!*" However, if someone is given a choice, the seven principles will come into play. For example, if you recommend a high-end color-protection shampoo and cost is an issue for your client, she may not purchase that particular shampoo. However, if you also carry a medium or lower priced product line, the client may purchase one of those options because it is more economical.

Chapter Seven

Bull's-Eye

So, let's review briefly.

We have determined that:

1. You are a professional in a professional industry.
2. People buy and use beauty products.
3. You have a goal to sell retail products.
4. You have a responsibility to recommend products.
5. You are focused on your goal.
6. You understand how people decide what to buy.

So, who are you going to sell to? Who would be a good retail target? Hmmm … Let's ponder this for a second … Time's up!

In order to answer those questions, you must first ask yourself these questions:

1. Who walks into your salon?
2. Who washes their hair?
3. Who conditions their hair?
4. Who have you performed a chemical service on?
5. Who styles their hair?
6. Who has manicure and pedicure services?
7. Who has facials?

And here is the bonus question:

Who has hair, skin, or nails?

Hold on now . . . This answer might surprise you. Are you ready?

The answer:

Everyone!

Every single solitary person who sets foot through your door should be considered a target. This includes the mail carrier, delivery person, other sales reps, family, friends—and most especially, me! If I walk into your salon, please talk to me about the products that you carry.

Think about it. If you see sixty clients in a week (1.5 clients per hour for forty hours) and you sold one five-dollar item to each one, your additional income, based on national averages, would be:

60 clients per week × $5 purchase = $300 in weekly retail sales

**$300 × 23 percent (national average profit)
= $69 in additional weekly income**

$69 × 52 weeks per year = $3,588 in additional annual income

Knock, knock!

Who's there?

Opportunity!

And we all know that when opportunity knocks, you should *open the door*!

I had a stylist tell me once that every time opportunity knocked, her door was locked and she couldn't find the key. I very gently replied, *"Kick the cotton-pickin' thing down!"*

I don't care if you open a window, bust the door down, burn the door down, make a new hole in the wall, whatever, but you must take hold of the opportunity. Seize it!

Okay, okay, okay, I can hear the grumbling from here. I know not every client is going to purchase. I understand that. What I want you to understand is the *potential*. Yes, you can potentially sell to *every single client*.

All right then, let's look at it from a different angle:

National averages show that at least one-third of salon clients actually purchase products in salon. However, those averages also reveal that the average client purchases three products (shampoo, conditioner, and styling product). Also, the average cost of three products is around thirty-six dollars.

So, does that mean you should sell to fewer people? *No, no, no!* Bad train of thought! You *offer* retail products to *all* of your clients. This scenario just follows what national sales statistics show.

Look at it this way:

20 clients (who purchase) × $36 (average retail ticket) = $720 in weekly retail sales

$720 × 23 percent (national average profit) = $165.60 in additional weekly income

$165.60 × 52 weeks per year = $8,611.20 in additional income annually

Are you with me yet?
I don't know about you, but I sure could use an extra $8,600 per year. If you haven't already thought about it, let me just say that right now might be a good time to go back and look at the financial goals you set for yourself earlier.

Oh, by the way, the amount we concluded in the second illustration is indeed *$5,000.00 higher* than in the first illustration. So, now do you see how much higher your income could become if you apply just a few simple techniques?

Keep this in mind also: these numbers are based on national sales statistics—that is, the numbers are based on people who are *not trying or trained to sell.*

Chapter Eight

Okeydokey ... What Now?

Eleven Steps to Completing the Service

Now that we understand that we are professionals and that we have the right and responsibility to sell products; we have goals, focus, and the desire to succeed; we understand why people buy; and we know that everyone who walks into our salon is a target, what now?

You might be asking, "When and where do I begin?" You begin as soon as your client walks in the door. (Highlight or underline each of the **bold** points listed below.) Later, as you work through the "Tips and Snips" chapter, you will be able to create your own cheat sheet.

1. Greet the client in the lobby/retail area.

Do not yell across the room. Give them time to look around. My biggest pet peeve upon entering someplace new is that the employees think everyone should know where everything is automatically. Guess what? I don't know, and I won't know until someone shows me or I go on a mission to find out.

Introduce your clients to your business. Show them the retail area, the shampoo area, and areas for facials, massages, waxing and nails, if you have them. (Plant the seed for additional services they may need.) Show them where the coffee or beverage area is (and get them something to drink). Show them where the Internet access area or style books, magazines, and newspapers are. (It's a great idea to have a computer set up with Internet access or Wi-Fi. That way while clients are processing or if you are late, they can check their e-mail or news headlines.) Above all, for goodness' sake, show them where the bathroom is.

Introduce clients to the owner or manager (if it is not you) if he or she is available. This makes clients feel more comfortable.

Lead each client to your chair, seat and drape him or her, and then move to the next step.

2. Begin the five-minute consultation.

Ask the client questions about her hair. My favorite (thank you, Connie, for this little gem!) is "When was the last time you liked your hair?" You would be surprised at the number of people who get a dreamy look on their face, sigh, and say, "Oh, I loved my hair in 1985." (And do not, I repeat, *do not* double over laughing because you remember what *your* hair looked like in 1985!)

Find out what it was that the client liked so much about her hair back then. Maybe it *was* the style (retro is in!), or the color or how thick it was. Whatever the reason, this will give you clues as to what products and services to offer.

Ask what your client is looking for in a style. Does she want something classic, spunky, or in between? How much time does she want to spend styling it? I also want to add here that when your client has a picture of what she wants or tells you something she wants that you *know* is not going to look good on her, you better tell her no and explain why. When you are up front and honest with your clients, they will appreciate you more.

I was meeting my friend Pam after work for dinner one night, so I went to the salon where she worked to pick her up. When I got there, she told me she had a last-minute client coming for a haircut. She said it shouldn't take long and we would be out the door in thirty minutes. "Sweet," I said, "because I'm hungry!"

When Pam's client arrived, I had a seat in the waiting area, where I could hear the conversation and see Pam's face. Pam began her consultation with her client, and when she asked what the client had in mind for a style, the client began to explain how she wanted her hair.

As I said, I could see Pam's face—and it was hilarious! As the client was explaining what she wanted, Pam was shaking her head no. When the client was done explaining, I heard Pam say "So, that's what you're thinking?" The client responded, "Yes!" I saw Pam pat her on the back as she said, "Well, that was a nice thought!" I almost burst out laughing.

Pam then went on to explain, "You see, the goal of every hair stylist is to make every client look like they have the perfect-shaped face. If we do what you are thinking, it will make your jaw look really wide, and your nose look larger. Is that what you want?" Of course, her client said, "No!" So Pam went on to explain what she thought the client would look good with (plus color, highlights, manicure, and pedicure).

Three and a half hours (and one pizza I had to go get) later, this client was transformed. She looked great! The best part of the story is that she still drives two and a half hours to come see Pam, every eight weeks, and has been doing that for the last ten years!

Ask your clients what products they are currently using at home: shampoo, conditioner, styling products, body wash, skin care line, makeup, nail care line. And don't forget the tools: combs, brushes, picks, pins, ponytail holders, blow dryers, curling irons, flat irons, and hot rollers. Make notes on <u>everything</u> they tell you.

By the way, Pam's client left with $400 in retail that night!

3. Do an analysis based on the answers to the above questions.

If a client is using an over-the-counter brand of shampoo or conditioner, scrape the wax off her hair and show it to her. If she is using her appliances improperly, show her the damage on the ends of her hair. Pull a strand out and do elasticity and porosity tests.

4. Take your client to the shampoo bowl and get him or her comfortable.

At this point you have the client's undivided attention. Begin explaining what products you are using and why. Rephrase what you discussed in your consultation. "I am using ... because you told me ..." Also, explain the proper usage of the product, for example, "Squeeze out a dime size amount, emulsify well, and work through the hair ..." Make sure you give the client the opportunity to sample the fragrance and see the bottle. Make comments like, "You will love it because ..." and "You'll appreciate this because ..."

Understand the features and benefits of the products you offer. Here is a simple way to understand the difference. A *feature* is a fact. A *benefit* is what's in it for the client. The *bridge* is a statement that links the two and uses the word *you*.

Here's a quick example:

"This product is sulfate free [feature], *which you will love because* [bridge] *it won't fade your color* [benefit].

Another question I get a lot from stylists is "What products should I use on the back bar?" My honest opinion is that every salon should carry at least two or three lines (preferably three). Have a small economical line, a medium-sized/priced line, and a high end or exclusive line. Use your high end on back bar, *because it is easier to down sell than up sell*. If price becomes an issue, you can always show a lower-priced item that is professional and works (see more on this in segment 8).

5. When returning to the chair, verify what they are looking for in a style, color, perm, etc.

Listen for major hints on what products to use. Always, always, always reiterate what they have told you: "You told me you wanted ..." That way, one of three things will happen:

- Your client will know that you did listen to them and that you understand what they want.
- You can ensure that if you did not understand what they meant (a quarter-inch off instead of a quarter-inch left), you can correct it *before* starting.

- You'll find out if they've changed their mind between the shampoo bowl and the chair. Someone could walk by with a style the client likes. Or she may see a new poster. Or the client may just change her mind.

6. Now here is the fun part! The "who's yer" conversation.

I'm from the South, so I actually talk like this! I don't know about you, but when I'm doing a service, I need to concentrate. I have a hard time talking and doing a service at the same time because I talk with my hands. Ask the questions and get them started talking. People like to talk about themselves, so ask:

> "Who's yer employer?
> "Who's yer momma?
> "Who's yer daddy?
> "Who's yer spouse?
> "Who's yer kids?

Play twenty questions, I spy, or who's who. Ask the questions they will answer. But please don't get started in on yourself and all your problems. They don't like you that much yet. If you are cutting a friend's hair, just remember this: you are one bad haircut away from losing your friend.

The great Douglas A. Cox, while speaking to a group of stylists in Plymouth, Minnesota, gave this little gem of advice: "Take fifteen minutes a day to read. Five minutes to read something spiritual, five minutes to read something newsworthy, and five minutes to read something funny. That way, no matter who parks himself or herself in your chair, you will have something to talk to them about."

Keep clients talking about themselves; they should feel like the center of your universe for the time they are in your chair. Take notes on things they tell you; that way, when they come back, you will have something to get them started talking (their vacations, their kids' activities, new jobs, and so on) Also, write down some of the important events they may want you to do their hair or nails for; you will need to pre-book those appointments.

7. Once the cut is complete and you begin styling, explain what you are using, why, and how.

Place the bottle in your client's hands as you explain; that way they can see what it looks like, sample the fragrance, and feel the product. Ask the client how she likes the fragrance, and for Pete's sake, use the term *fragrance*. The word *smell* implies something negative. "Wow, that really smells!"

The senses are a very powerful selling tool, and in some situations … not! For example, someone could have something in a cup that smells horrible. If they stand in front of you, take a big whiff, say, "Oh! That smells terrible!" and then hand the cup to you, what would you do? You would take a big whiff, make an ugly face, and say, "Yeah, you're right!"

I'm assuming we do this because misery loves company. But we like to share enjoyable experiences as well. So, by the same token, if someone says, "This has a fabulous fragrance!" We will want to check that out as well. (I, however, have learned not to fall into the trap of smelling something terrible. If someone offers it up, I just say, "No, thank you. That is not a memory I need.")

8. Ask for the sale.

"We have these products in stock so you can take them home with you today." Again, guarantee your services *only* if clients purchase professional retail products from you. They can tell you they use professional products all day long, but what they are actually using and what they *say* they use are usually two totally different things.

Case in point: I had a client that I did a triple process color on, who swore up and down that she used professional products. I was new in the industry, so—newbie that I was—I believed her. Well she was back in the salon a week later, because that $250 color had faded to an ugly duckling gray. Whoa! What happened? Well, bless her heart, all she did was shampoo and condition with her "professional products" when she got home. Uh-huh. And what was the name of those products? Well, let's just say there is a national TV commercial that says something along the lines of "If you have flakes, your stylist *would recommend it." Ha! Not this stylist! Know why? Because it strips color!*

If a client says no to your product suggestion, there are three things you need to do:

1. Clarify the objection. Find out why the client is saying no. Does she not like the product itself? Is it the fragrance or the price?
2. Offer a secondary recommendation or a package. Explain any package deals or promotions you have going on to help put the product in the client's hands.
3. Down sell if you must. If price is the client's only objection, then explain that that is why you have more than one product offering. (Remember, I explained earlier that you want to have two or three lines available, if for no other reason than price objections.) The other thing to do is explain that you would rather them "have one than none." So, if they have received a color service, the most important product for them would be a color-preserve shampoo. If they received a cut, the most important product is the styling product you used. If it was a perm, they need a great conditioner.

9. Remember to up sell.

My favorite question to ask at this point is "Is one enough?" More than likely, you will get the ol' deer in the headlights look when you ask this, so follow it with, "Who do you know that could benefit from this product?" Now, I have to tell you, my friend Connie suggested we start asking those questions in the salon. At first I thought she was crazy—you really have to work hard to sell retail, right?

I have to say that the first time I used those questions, the results were phenomenal. Those two questions get your clients thinking about every person they know. The first time I asked it was thirty days before Christmas. My client's eyes lit up, and she said, "You know, this stuff would make great Christmas presents!" Absolutely! By the time she got done, her total product purchase was over $350.

Also, remember that the average retail size product will only last four to six weeks with daily usage. If your client is booking out longer than six weeks, she will need more than one container each of shampoo, conditioner, and styling aid. But they won't know that unless you tell them.

Find out who will be using the product. Is it just for the client, or will his or her spouse be using it too? Will the kids be using it? Will they use it on their dog? Yes, I know—laugh all you want. But remember, many people that have little dogs do baby them. It's just as important to ask how many bathrooms they have. If the whole family is using the products and they have two bathrooms at their house, guess what? They'll need a set for each bathroom.

Don't be afraid of larger sizes. In this industry, a bonus size (or liter) is simply a license to use more. If you will consider spending the extra couple of dollars for liter pumps, your clients will be back sooner than you think. The reason for this is that they will use a full pump every single time. Even when you tell them to use less, they will always use more. Let them!

10. Thank the client for her business and schedule her next appointment.

I cannot stress this enough. Show a little appreciation for your clients; they will be back. They will get into the habit of pre-booking. They will listen when you prescribe professional products. Yes, I use the term *prescribe*. That should be what you are doing. Again, we go back to completing the service.

Keep in mind that you want to pre-book their next three appointments. Here is why: if they have their next three appointments scheduled with you already, they know if they change one, they will have to change all of them. They will then schedule everything else around you.

11. Accept tips graciously.

To me this is probably one of the most overlooked steps in the process of dealing with your clients. In my capacity as a salon consultant, I have seen some pretty ugly tip accepting. I have seen stylists decline tips because they thought they should be higher. I've seen stylists look at tips and say very sarcastically, "Gee, thanks."

I need you to understand what tips are. A tip is over and above what that client thinks you are worth. The stylist that does my hair does a fabulous job to begin with. She squeezes me in when I need to get in. She bends over backward for me and then tries to give me my tip back because she thinks it is too much. Stop it! Many of the clients I have talked to say that when the stylist makes a big deal out of how much the tip is, they actually find it offensive.

And now ...

The service is complete.

Chapter Nine

Set, Go!

When I began writing this book, my son had just turned two. His favorite thing to say before doing something he was unsure of was "Set, go!" Then he would just go for it. There was no "On your mark … get ready" to it. Just "Set, go!"

If you want to be truly successful in retailing in the salon, just close your eyes and jump with both feet. Step outside your comfort zone and try. As the saying goes, "If at first you don't succeed, try, try again."

The question is never "Do you need anything today?" It's "What problem can I solve today?" As it pertains to skin, hair, and nails, remember this:

QOCE

QOCE is **q**uality **of** **c**lient **e**xperience. Take good care of them, and they will take care of you.

It is my sincere hope that you have had as much fun reading this as I had writing it.

Try to utilize this information every day. Don't just try it one day and then quit if you don't succeed right away. This is not a diet.

I have included some helpful forms and quick reference information in the "Tips and Snips" chapter to assist you with getting started setting retail goals and achieving them.

God bless!

Chapter Ten

Tips and Snips

In this section I have included some of the information we offer on the Transformations Salon Consulting website. This information is designed to help you track your goals for service and retail sales.

Weekly Gross Sales Per Station
Hourly Services Average
Percentage of Pre-books
Retail Sales Goal
SMART Goal Setting
Goal Plan Worksheet
Promotional Plan Directions
Promotion Plan Worksheet
Eleven Steps to Completing the Service (cheat sheet)

All of this information and more can be obtained by going to the TSC website (www.salontransformations.com) and becoming a member.

Chapter 6 - Why Do People Buy? Answer Key:

7. Price
6. Product warranty
5. Satisfaction guaranty
4. Convenience
3. Selection
2. Quality
1. Service!

Weekly Gross Sales Per Station

To calculate what each station and/or treatment area should be making in income to keep your business afloat, use the following formula:

Enter:

1. Total monthly expenses $_____
   Enter ALL of your monthly fixed and variable expenses together on this line

2. Projected monthly profit $_____
   Enter the amount of profit you WANT to make each month on this line; average profit is 10 to 20 percent over expenses.

3. Enter the number of stations $_____
   Add all stations and treatment rooms in the salon/spa.

Calculate:

4. Total projected gross sales $_____
   Add lines 1 and 2 and enter on this line.

5. Station/treatment room cost $_____
   Divide line 4 by line 3 and enter here.

6. Weekly gross sales $_____
   Divide line 5 by the number on line 4 to give you the weekly gross totals.

This number is the absolute number you have to make per week, per station, to stay in business!

Hourly Services Average (HSA)

Now that we have determined the amount you need to make weekly, you must next determine the amount you need to average hourly to reach that goal. This is also how you are going to determine your prices!

Weekly gross sales per station _____
Divided by average operation hours _____
Equals your target HSA _____

By calculating your HSA you now know what you need to make hourly to reach your weekly gross sales goal. To set prices, make sure the HSA is *at minimum* what you charge for basic services.

Example: If your HSA is thirty-five dollars and you charge sixteen dollars for a haircut and you average two haircuts per hour, you need to raise your hair cut prices to $17.50. Additionally, if it takes you two hours to do a perm or color, your minimum price for those services should be seventy dollars (two hours multiplied by thirty-five dollars per hour).

Percentage of Pre-books

You always want to know the number of pre-booked clients you see in a week. This number will eventually determine when you do a major price increase. To calculate these numbers follow this formula:

Number of pre-booked clients this week _____
Divided by total number of clients _____
Equals your pre-book percentage _____

Once your percentage hits 80 percent, it's time to raise your prices! In general, you want to consistently raise your prices to keep up with rising prices elsewhere. However, once you hit an 80 percent pre-book rate, raise prices just to give yourself a raise. You deserve it!

Retail Sales Goal

Average number of clients per week: _____
    (Include all clients)

Average service ticket: _____
    (Total receipts for services ÷ avg. number of clients)

Average total weekly gross service sales: = _____
    (Avg. # of clients × Avg. service ticket)

Retail to service percentage target: _____ percent
    (Set this number to what you wish to achieve)

Dollar retail goal per week: = _____
    (Avg. total weekly gross service sales × _____ percent)

Dollar retail goal per client: = _____
    (Dollar retail goal per week ÷ avg. number of clients)

Your goal is to sell $_____ worth of retail to *every* client.

By utilizing this formula you will be able to determine the amount of retail you need to sell to maintain your retail-to-service ratio goals. These numbers must be tracked weekly to determine if the established goals are being met.

SMART Goal Setting

The SMART system is an easy way to remember the basics of goal setting. SMART stands for:

Specific: The goal should be specifically about one area.
Measurable: The success of the goal should be measured in increments.
Attainable: Never set your goals out of reach.
Result oriented: Build your goal around the end result.
Time-sensitive: Set a date by which you want the goal completed.

There are seven components to a written goal. Once you have made up your mind about what you wish to achieve, break it down further into the seven individual components:

1. State the goal using SMART guidelines.
   What are you going to achieve?
2. State the benefit of achieving the goal.
   How will you benefit from reaching your goal?
3. State the obstacles or barriers.
   Is there anyone or anything that stands in the way?
4. State any additional skills or knowledge you will need.
   Will you need any additional training to succeed?
5. State who you will work with.
   Is there someone who can assist you?
6. Stick with it—do not rewrite.
   If you find yourself not reaching the goal, keep trying!
7. Set an end date and list consequences.
   When do you want to achieve the goal by—and what happens if you don't make it?

Once you have completed your worksheets, make at least four copies. Keep one with you at all times (in your wallet, on a photo keychain, or in your address book, for example). Put two where you will see them every day. I always recommend the bathroom mirror and the refrigerator door because these are two places we are always looking. Finally, give a copy to someone you trust (like your spouse, parent, pastor, teacher, boss, or best friend), who will help hold you accountable.

Goal Plan
"A goal without a plan is a wish."

"Where there is no vision, the people perish."
—Proverbs 29:18 (KJV)

Goal _____
_____
_____
_____
_____

Benefit_____
_____
_____
_____
_____

Obstacles or Barriers_____
_____
_____
_____
_____

Additional Skills or Knowledge_____
_____
_____
_____
_____

Who I Will Work With_____
_____
_____
_____
_____

End Date _____

Consequence _____

Signed Commitment _____

Today's Date _____

NOTES:

Promotional Plan Directions

The purpose of the promotion-plan worksheet is to assist you in planning your promotions for optimum results.

To run a proper promotion you must plan ahead! Six to twelve weeks in advance, begin using this worksheet to plan what you are going to do and how you are going to do it.

DATES - Begin with a start and end date. Do not start the promotion prior to these dates. Make sure your end date is the actual *end* date. For best results, plan to run the promotion for six to eight weeks. The reason for this is so that all of your clients have an opportunity to take advantage of the promotion.

THEME - Will there be a theme to the promotion? For example, if the promotion centers around a holiday, make sure your decorations are appropriate. This should include posters, shelf talkers, mirror clings, and stylist attire.

SPECIAL - What will the promotion be about? Is it a service special, a retail special, or both? What will the cost savings to your clients be—a percentage or a fixed dollar amount off?
Will there be any additional incentive?

INCENTIVE - This is a twofold category. Will there be an additional incentive for your clients? For example, if a client takes advantage of the promotion, will his or her name go in for a drawing for a grand prize? Also, don't forget about your stylists. Offer them an incentive for selling the promotion to their clients.

GOAL - What do you want to achieve with this promotion? Do you want to increase retail and/or service sales? By what percentage? Make sure you have a goal set; otherwise you will never know if it is successful or not.

MARKETING - How are you going to get your clients in the door for this promotion? Which media advertising are you going to use? Newspaper, radio, flyers, word of mouth, or the web? To make a promotion successful, you need two things: a good viable promotion and someone to purchase it.

BUDGET - This is very important. Make sure you have a budget for everything. Decorations, incentives, retail stock, back bar stock, food, and drinks. Don't forget to include any plates, napkins, and flatware in your decorations budget.

TRACKING - Once the promotion is complete, deduct all expenses from the total promotion sales to see if it was a success or not. This will help you to determine whether this is a promotion you will want to try again.

Promotion Plan

DATES _____

THEME _____
_____
_____
_____
_____

SPECIAL _____
_____
_____
_____
_____

INCENTIVE _____
_____
_____
_____
_____

GOAL _____
_____
_____
_____
_____

MARKETING _____
_____
_____
_____
_____

BUDGET _____

_____

_____

_____

_____

Eleven Steps to Completing the Service

Here is where you are going to create your own "Completing the Service" cheat sheet. Take a few minutes and write the steps highlighted in chapter 8, "Okeydokey … What Now?" Writing this information down after reading it will help you retain more of it.

Once you have completed this, cut it out and keep it in your station. That way you have a constant reminder to talk to your clients about the products that you are using.

---

11 Steps to Completing the Service

1. _____

2. _____

3. _____

4. _____

5. _____

6. _____

7. _____

8. _____

9. _____

10. _____

11. _____